GW01551528

Sunshine Onset Teacher's Notes

Frances James

Contents

Introduction

Activities

Photocopiable masters

Letter Blend Knowledge recording grid

Introduction

In recent years there has been considerable debate about how children become accurate, fluent readers. There is now, however, a general consensus that children need to develop skills associated with the visual, context and phonological cognitive processors. The visual processor allows readers to recognise whole words by sight, the context processor provides the meaning of the text and the phonological processor relates the written symbols (letters) to their associated sounds. This book and the associated reading books focus on an important aspect of phonological development.

The largest units of sounds, associated with listening, are words. Words can be divided into different units of sounds – syllables, onsets, rimes and phonemes. Syllables are denoted by specific rhythms within words. Within syllables there are rimes and onsets. The rime is the final sequence of letters that allow it to rhyme with other words or syllables, the onset is the initial letter or sequence of letters in the syllable. Phonemes are the smallest units of sound. There are 44 phonemes in English. Phonemes have different graphic representations or spelling choices. For example – **c**at, **k**itten, **Ch**ristmas are all different graphic representations of the same phoneme.

Summary of phonological units

Word	Syllable(s)	Onset	Rime	Phonemes
cat	cat	c	at	c – a – t
chair	chair	ch	air	ch – ai – r
bathroom	bath	b	ath	b – a – th
	room	r	oom	r – oo – m

Research indicates that children develop phonological awareness through a broadly developmental sequence – starting with the largest phonological units, words, and eventually developing an accurate appreciation of the smallest units, phonemes. This knowledge of phonemes allows children to read and spell unknown words. Important steps in the acquisition of working knowledge of phonemes are an appreciation of syllables and rhyme and alliteration. Recognition and appreciation of alliteration – words that share the same sounds at the beginning – is important. With this knowledge children will learn that words that share similar spelling patterns will frequently sound alike. This knowledge will assist their spelling as they develop a sense of analogy.

This book and the associated texts focus on developing children's appreciation of alliteration and onsets – specifically consonant blends and digraphs. Consonant blends are common combinations of consonants – for example *b* and *r*. It is possible to hear the individual phonemes within the blends. Digraphs are two consonants that, combined together, are a graphic representation of a phoneme; in other words they represent one single sound. Examples of digraphs are *th–*, *sh–*, *ch–* and *wh–*.

With an appreciation of these onsets children will begin to gain knowledge of word families and to recognise that by substituting the rimes they will be able to generate new words. For example, by changing the *ick* of *stick* with *ill,* a new word *still* is made. This knowledge is an excellent introduction to essential reading and reading skills.

The Literacy Hour

In the National Literacy Strategy, three distinct strands of reading instruction are identified – the word, sentence and text levels. *Sunshine Phonics* focuses on the word level, which contributes to children's knowledge of phonics, spelling and vocabulary. However, the books can also be used to develop aspects of text and sentence work, as the onsets are presented in meaningful text and there is a strong emphasis upon enhancing children's comprehension.

The *Sunshine Onset and Rime Books* address two key teaching objectives identified in the National Literacy Strategy:

- build words with different initial clusters by analogy in rhyming sets;
- break words into parts and use phonemic spelling to build up syllabic spelling patterns.

The books also cover many of the specific phonics and spelling work in line with the National Literacy Strategy recommendations for Years 1 to 4.

The reading books and associated materials may be used for whole class teaching, group or individual work – all of which are advocated as appropriate teaching approaches in the Literacy Hour.

How to introduce the Onset Reading Books

Introduce the book by showing the class or group of children the cover. Draw the children's attention to the picture on the cover and talk about what the story might be about. Ask the children to read the title of the book. Discuss other aspects of the cover, including the name of the author and illustrator.

If the title contains two or more alliterative words write up the onset so that the children can see it. Ask individual children to come out and point out the alliterative words. Encourage detailed study of the words – which letters do the words have in common and which letters are different? Let the children name the letters in the blend or digraph in sequence. Blend the onsets and the rimes of the words with the children. Ensure that the children articulate the blends and digraphs correctly and that they do not distort them – for example, pronouncing the *st* in *sticks* as *ster*. When the children articulate the blends or phonemes encourage them to reflect on the position of their tongue and the shape of their mouth as they say them.

Ask the children to think of other words that belong to the same alliteration family and write them for the children to study. The children may suggest words that alliterate but do not share the same spelling pattern – for example when talking about *ski, skip* and *skate* the children might suggest *scarf* or *scarecrow*. Praise their suggestions and tell them that they have identified the blends of the right phoneme but that those words have a different spelling. Write the words down away from the target word blend family so that they can see the difference. This approach introduces the children to the idea that there are spelling choices in English.

Let the children read the book with you as a group or individually. Sometimes it is a good idea to read the story to the children first, acting as a reading model, emphasising the alliterative words and appropriate intonation. Talk about the story, relating it to the children's own experience wherever possible. Ensure that the children understand all the vocabulary in the books, either by introducing key words before the book is read or by careful questioning after the book is finished. Develop the children's comprehension and vocabulary by using open-ended questions – ones that demand more than a one-word answer.

Children should be given the opportunity to reread the books frequently. This will give them the chance to reinforce their phonological skills and to build up their automatic recognition of words – which characterises a competent reader. Ensure that the Onset Readers are readily accessible to the children – make them part of regular book displays and incorporate them into topic work where appropriate. Let the children read the books as a shared or paired reading activity. The children may also read the books to volunteers in the class, to younger children, or record them to make up a bank of class cassettes.

Using the Teacher's Notes

For 20 selected books there are teacher's notes. These notes contain ideas of how to develop specific phonological skills related to the target blend or digraph. Many of the ideas and activities can be adapted for use with other onsets and alliteration families. The teacher's notes also have ideas for linking the books with writing activities and for developing the children's appreciation of the story. The words belonging to the blend or digraph family which are in the text are identified in the teacher's notes.

For each of the books the teacher's notes has a short poem with words containing the target blend or digraph. These poems may be used in a variety of ways. Use them to reinforce the alliterative words in the reading books. Write them out to make a class collection for the children to read and to illustrate. Teach the children the poem, encouraging them to identify the alliterative words. If the children recite the poem as a group observe all the children carefully to check that individual children are not just "mouthing" the words.

Activity Sheets

The 20 selected texts have an associated activity sheet for the children to complete. These sheets promote a multi-sensory approach to reinforce the onsets. The children are required to write selected words from the word families. As they write, encourage them to recite the names of the letters to consolidate their memory of the letter sequences.

Children who find the work more challenging should be provided with magnetic or plastic letters whilst they do the activity sheets. This will allow them to make the words before they write them and will promote their appreciation of analogy – by replacing the onset it is possible to make new words in the same word family.

When the children have completed the activity sheets, ensure that they read them either to you or a friend – this work is essentially about the sounds within words and so it is important that the children constantly refer back to the similarities they can hear in the words. Draw their attention to the onsets that they have used.

Links with home

Encourage the children to take the books home to share with members of their family. You may wish to write a short explanation for the children's parents and carers about why the knowledge of alliteration is important in the development of children's reading and spelling skills and ways in which they can support this – for example, learning tongue twisters, sharing alphabet books, playing "I Spy" and riddles with their child. Develop banks of appropriate books which the families can borrow to support this work.

By Ann Wilson
Illustrations by Janet Cowood

Words featured

brown
bring

Poem

Brown Bricks

Brush the old brown
    bricks.
Brush them with a
    broom.
Brush them 'til they're
    brighter,
Brighter than the moon.

John Lockyer

Brrrrr! Brown Bear

Skill Development

1. Read the title and write it up in large letters: ask the children:
   • Why is *Brrrrr!* written like that?
2. Read the story together.
   • Focus on the text, locating all the words that begin with *br*.
   • Emphasise the beginning sound throughout. Ask children to put a circle with their fingers around the blend.
3. Children reread the story by themselves.
   • They read the word bank at the back of the book independently.
4. Make a set of large cards, featuring words beginning with *br*.
   • Laminate and use with whiteboard markers so children can write the words.
   • Encourage the children to name the letters as they write.
5. List some words beginning with *br* on a magnetic board using plastic magnetic letters.

Writing

1. Write rhymes together featuring words beginning with *br*.
   • Put them in the class poetry collection.
2. Reread the *br* chart made previously with the children.
3. Create a class or group mural depicting situations which make the children say "brrrr!"
   • Children could write their stories in speech bubbles.

4. With the children, write a number of sentences featuring words beginning with *br*.
   • Cut these up for the children to mix and match sentences with.
5. Ask the children to listen to the sounds of the words as you blend them together: *br–own*; *br–ush*.
   • What word you are saying?
   • Ask them to put the sounds back together.

Develop the story

1. Ask the children to:
   • make charts to show how they keep warm in the winter, then illustrate them using magazine pictures.
   • draw a selection of winter and summer clothing in two piles under labels saying "Brrr!" and "Phew!"
   • explore books in the library to find out how animals survive the winter and present their findings in a class mural, booklet or big book to share.

Crazy Crocodile

Onset Books

By Clare Scott
illustrations by Astrid Matijasevic

Skill development

1. Read the story together:
   - Focus on the text, locating all the words that begin with *cr*.
   - Find them in the written text and at the back of the book.
   - Dramatise words like *crunching, crawling, creep* to reinforce meaning. Check that the children understand all the words.
2. Children create a simple web of all the words beginning with *cr*.
3. Children share in writing words and illustrating a large index.
   - Read the story a number of times as the index is created.
   - Children can make black felt marker drawings to illustrate the index.

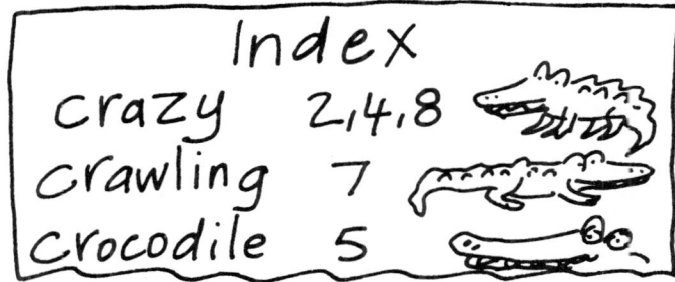

4. Play "Odd one out" game using the blend cards.
   - Show three cards. Children guess which is the odd one out.
5. Children collect or draw objects beginning with *cr* (a crumb, a cracker, a crisp, a crab, a cricket) and objects with names beginning with other letter combinations.
   - They identify the odd one out.

Writing

1. Write a new story called *Crunch some crackers!*
   - Include all the children in the class.

Develop the story

1. Present the story using a comic strip format.
   - Children write their names in the written text.
   - They illustrate the new story with pictures of themselves crunching crackers.
   - Children write *Crunch! Crunch! Crunch!* in speech bubbles following the model presented in *Crazy Crocodile*.

Words featured

crazy
crocodile
crunching
crunch
crawling
creek
creep

Poem

Crocodile Crunch

What do crocodiles
eat for lunch?
Crisps and crackers
and cream cakes.
Crunch, crunch, crunch.

Jane Buxton

Onset Teacher's Notes

By Ruth Corrin
Illustrations by Richard Hoit

Onset Books

Words featured

fruggles
fruggle
fridge
friend
Fred
frozen
from
frost
freezing

Poem

Frostbite

I've frostbite in my
    fingers.
I've frostbite in my toes.
I'm frightened that my
    freck es
Will be frozen on my
    nose!

Susan Frame

Fruggles

Skill Development

1. Read the story together.
   • Children identify the *fr* words. Discuss their meaning.
   • Children give examples of other words that begin with *fr*.
2. Make a chart or word bank of words beginning with *fr*
   • Ask the children to illustrate this.
3. Children read the story by themselves.
   • They use the word bank to read the words one by one.
4. Make *fr* words using magnetic letters on a magnetic board.
5. Children illustrate the chart made during the introduction as an independent activity.
6. Children listen to the sounds of each word as you say it: *fr–idge*.
   • Ask what word you said.
   • Make it a game by asking children to take turns doing the same thing.
7. Make a flip chart highlighting the letter blend.

Writing

In a shared writing session, write some rhymes or poems featuring words beginning with *fr*.
1. Write a class poem using the word bank words at the back of the book:
   • Friendly Fruggles; frozen friend; fridge freezer; frosty Fred.
2. Model a story map on the whiteboard.
   • Ask the children to create their own story maps.
3. Ask the children to draw Fruggles or his friends.

Develop the story

1. Children illustrate the rhymes and poems.
   • Ask them to paste them onto card to use as an independent reading activity.
2. Children retell the story or poem on tape.
3. Children role play the story to a group or the class.
4. Children draw or make collage pictures of friends for Fruggles for a class book.
5. Research library or classroom books for other words beginning with *fr*.
6. Make up some other nonsense words like Fruggles beginning with *fr*.
   e.g. fricicle, fricies.
   • Write stories together using these names.

Granny Green

Skill Development

1. Read the title of the story, emphasising the *gr* blend.
   - Write it up in large letters so the children can see it.
2. Ask the children what other words they know that start with *gr*.
   - Write them on a web chart.
   - Children listen to and say the words as they are written.

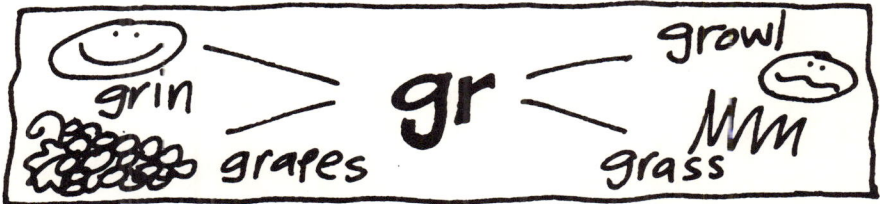

3. Read the story together.
   - Children find all the words beginning with *gr*.
   - Add them to the web and say them with the children.
4. Discuss personal experiences of grandparents.
   - What are other words for grandfather and grandmother?
5. Children read the story by themselves.
   - they use the word bank to read the words one by one.
6. Make words beginning with *gr* using magnetic letters on a magnetic board.
7. Children illustrate the word bank they made during the introduction.
8. Listen to the sounds in the words.
   - Children say the sounds with you.
   - Write them up and read them: *gr–in, grin–ning; growl, growl–ing.*

Writing

1. Write a new story about Granny or Grandpa Green.
   - Use the same refrain but think of different things to use in the story. For example: *Grandpa Green can't find his slippers. He is happy when Granny Green finds them for him.*
2. Write a class poem incorporating *gr* words. For example:
   - Cabbages, spinach and peas are green
     How many green things have you seen?

Develop the story

1. Children illustrate their new story to make a big book for the class.
2. Children read the new story together.
3. Write the text of the original or new story on strips of cardboard.
   - Cut into separate words.
   - Children reassemble the sentences to match the text.

Words featured

Granny
Green
Grandpa
growling
grinning

Poem

Green Grass

I grow green grass,
I grow green grapes,
I also grow green pears.
I feed them all
to great grey sharks
And greedy grizzly bears.

John Carr

By Susan Frame
Illustrations by Liz McIntosh

Onset Books

Words featured

try
tractor
tree
trampoline
tricky
trumpet
trombone
tricks
tremendous
true

Poem

Trucks and Tractors

Trucks and tractors,
Trains and trams,
Traffic, traffic,
Traffic jams.

Ruth Corrin

Tricky Tricks

Skill Development

1. Read the story through. Children read the books for themselves for enjoyment and to spot words beginning with *tr*.
   - Children share what they have found by reading the sentence out loud.
   - Write the words using the letter blend *tr* for children to see. Say the words together.
   - Use a mask to reveal the patterns of the blend words. Children tell you the word when they recognise it.
   - Have a selection of books in which tricks have been played. Children share, read independently for enjoyment and identify the 'tricks'.
   - Make a mural depicting the poem

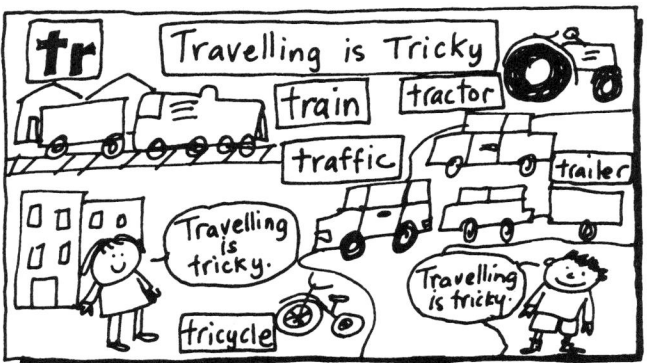

   - Blend the sounds. Say *tr–y*, *tr–actor*. Children say the words. Read the story again. Pause before words beginning with *tr* and ask children to read them.

Writing

1. Construct a class book about things the children 'try' to do, using words beginning with *tr*: 'I try tricky tricks on the trampoline.'
2. Children write and draw to create their own two-page books about all the things they try to do.

Develop the story

1. Make a wall display. Children draw and cut out self-portraits using felt-tips, crayons or paint.
   - Make cards with illustrations using words in the class word bank.

Cloudland

By Susan Frame
Illustrations by Jim Storey

Onset Books

Skill Development

1. Read the story together.
   - Talk about meaning.
2. Find all the words that begin with *cl* in the text.
   - Say them with the children.
   - Write them on a chart.
   - Ask the children to think of other words they can add.
3. Children read the story by themselves.
   - They read the words from the word bank one by one.
4. Use magnetic letters on a magnetic board to make words beginning with *cl*.
5. Read the chart made earlier with the children.
   - Ask them to illustrate it.
   - Display either as a chart or as a page to go in the class blend book.
6. Write the featured word on card, cutting the initial blend as indicated.
   - Children may use this as a word building activity, checking words with the text as they use them.

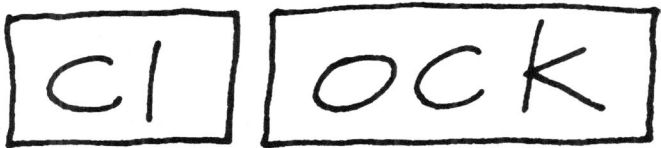

Writing

1. Take the children outside to look at the clouds.
   - Discuss and record their findings on a chart.
   - Make up a word bank.
   - Ask the children to record their observations, illustrate them and then present them in the following ways.

individual booklets   shaped stories   a mobile

2. In a shared writing activity, ask the children to:
   - Make and illustrate a shaped cloud poem for the class poetry box.
   - Use as many words as possible that begin with *cl*.

Develop the story

1. Observe the clouds every day for a week. Make up a concertina booklet.
   - Children can write a caption for observations noted each day:
     eg Monday: 'Today the clouds are white. We saw a clever clown.'
   - Make collage pictures using cotton wool or torn paper.
   - Write captions provided by the children.
2. Explore other books on the topic in the classroom or school library.

Words featured

clouds
clown
claws
clock
clothes
clarinet
climbing

Poem

Clever Cloud

The rain cloud washed
our classroom,
What a clever cloud!
Even the thunder
Was clapping very loud.

John Carr

Onset Books

By John Carr
Illustrations by Terry Burton

Words featured

flip
flap
flop
flowers
flag
floor

Poem

Fly

The fly flew off the floor,
To see what he could
        see.
But all he saw was a
        flower,
A flag, a flute and a flea.

Gavin Bishop

Flop, Flap, Flip

Skill Development

1. Ask the children what they know about penguins.
2. Read the title of the story, emphasising the *fl* sounds.
   - Guess what might happen in the story.
3. Ask what other words the children know that start with *fl*.
   - Write them up as a web for the children to see.
   - Listen to and say the words.
4. Read the story together.
   - Find all the words beginning with *fl*.
   - Add them to the web and say them with the children.
5. Make a flip chart for the blend *fl*.
6. Children reread the story by themselves.
   - They use the word bank at the back of the book to read the words one by one.
7. Play "Memory" (pelmanism) with the blend cards:
   - Lay all the cards face down.
   - Try to find the *fl* cards.
8. Oral blending:
   - Say the first sound.
   - Blend the other sounds with it: *fl–ip, fl–op*
9. Look at the alliteration in the story.
   - Write other sequences of 'sound' words that begin with the same letters: *drip, drop, drop.*

Writing

1. Write a new story using different *fl* words for the things that penguins might walk on.
2. Play a spelling game.
   - Say each word that begins with *fl*.
   - Write the blend.
   - Ask the children to listen to the last phonemes,
   - then spell the word: *fl–y.*
3. Make and break words starting with *fl* on a magnetic board.

Develop the story

1. Children illustrate the new story to make a concertina book.

   - Read the new story together.
   - Act out the new story in groups.
2. Make up a play altogether in the playground.
   - Children walk like penguins and say the words "flip, flap, flop", as they walk.
   - They walk backwards at the end, to help them understand the story clearly.

Glueing My Glider

By Jane Buxton
illustrations by Kelvin Hawley

Skill Development

1. Read the story together.
   - Identify the *gl* words.
   - Ask the children for other words that begin with *gl*.
   - Talk about the meaning of the words and the story.
   - Make a chart or word bank of words beginning with *gl* for children to illustrate later.
2. Children read the story by themselves.
   - They use the word bank to read the words one by one.
3. Make *gl* words using magnetic letters on a magnetic board, making and breaking the words to illustrate the *gl* sound.
4. Children illustrate the chart made during the introduction as an independent activity.
5. Ask children to tell you the odd word out in a sequence of words: *glue, glad, give*.
6. Children listen to the sounds in each word.
   - Ask them to tell you how many sounds they hear: *gl–ue, gl–ider*.

Writing

1. Write words beginning with gl on black paper using coloured PVA glue.
   - Sprinkle with glitter.
2. Children write their own versions of the story .
   - They use the pattern of the original and their own names: *There's glue on Tim's gloves*.
   - Then they write their own word bank.
   - Write the story in glove shapes.

Develop the story

1. Write text on strips of cardboard then cut up into separate words.
   - Children reassemble the sentences to match the text.
2. Make a cardboard glider.
   - Use simple directions and steps.
   - Sketch and label the components of the glider.

Words featured

glueing
glider
glue
glasses
gloves
glad

Poem

Gleam and Glint

There's a gleam in my
   smile.
There's a glint in my eye.
I'm glad to be
an eagle,
Gliding through
the sky.

John Carr

By John Carr

Illustrations by Barbara Vagnozzi

Onset Books

Words featured

plays
plane
plug
plank
plant
plate
plums
plonk

Poem

Plums

My Dad is cooking
purple plums,
purple plums with peas.
Can I stay at your place?
Please, please, please?

John Carr

The Mouse Plays With The Plane

Skill Development

1. Read the story, emphasising but not distorting the blend sounds at the beginning of each target word.
2. Ask the children for other words beginning with *pl*.
   • Make a class chart or word bank.
3. Listen to the sound words in the book.
   • Ask the children to tell you others.
   • Write them up: *plank, plonk, plink, plunk, play*.
   • Children can illustrate these sounds on the chart.
4. Children read the story by themselves.
   • They use the word bank to read the words one by one.
5. Children use coloured felt pens to highlight the blends on the class word chart.
6. Match the pictures and words in the blend card game to the words on the chart.
   • Add any that are not there.

Writing

1. Ask the children to:
   • draw and write themselves into a new story.
   • follow the same pattern as the book.

2. The children write the target words as labels.
   • They list them on the inside back cover, using the model in the book.
3. Children read their stories in a class sharing session.
   • Listen to the sounds, write the words and read them.
   • Recombine the sounds and say the words: *pl–ay; pl–ane; pl–as–tic*.

Develop the story

1. Create a wall display using the language from the story and the children's illustrations.
2. Write the text on strips of cardboard.
   • Cut up into separate words.
   • Children reassemble the sentences to match the text.

A Slimy Slug

Skill development

1. Ask the children what letters make the blend *sl* and write *sl* on a large sheet of paper.
   - How many other words do they know which have the *sl* sound?
   - Make a *sl* chart as they find more words.
   - Ask the children to draw pictures beside the words they write.
2. Read the story slowly, emphasising the *sl* words.
3. Ask the children to think of all the things the slug went on.
   - Write them up on the whiteboard.
4. Children read the story on their own.
   - Match the words in the word bank with the words in the story.
5. Children make their own cards with *sl* words.
   - Write the words and draw a picture.
   - Say the words that begin with *sl* slowly; *sl–eep*.
   - Ask the children to tell you the word.
   - Write the word so the children can see it and read it. Be careful that you do not distort the individual phonemes.
6. Play odd word out.
   - Ask the children to identify which word in a sequence does not begin with *sl*.

Writing

1. Ask the children to look carefully at the illustrations.
   - Talk about the leaves pointing downwards and how this helped the slug.
2. Draw a story map on the whiteboard.
   - Children draw and label their own story maps of the story.

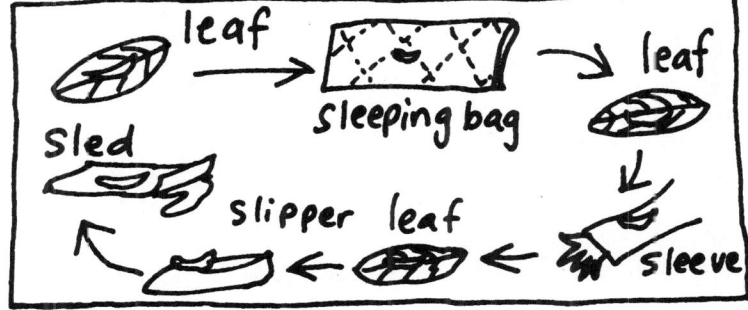

3. Break up the syllables of the words by saying them deliberately.
   - Ask how many syllables children can hear in words like *slug, slime, slimy, sleeping*.

Develop the story

1. Children write their own slimy slug story including the word bank at the back.
   - Ask them to take the booklets home to share with their family.
2. Children write "I Spy" charts featuring the *sl* blend.
   - Copy the poem *Slimy Slug* for the children to read on an overhead projector.
   - Children paint a picture of things that begin with the letters *sl*.

Words featured

slimy
slug
sleeping
slide
sleeve
slipper
sled

Poem

Slimy Slug

Slippery slimy slug
Sleeping in the dew.
You'd better slide away
   and hide
Before a bird eats you.

Jane Buxton

Onset Teacher's Notes

17

Onset Books

By Ruth Corrin

illustrations by Isabella Misso

Words featured

scarlet
scary
scared
scat

Poem

Scarecrow

Scaly Sam the scarecrow,
His hair full of hay,
Uses tricks from
    scarecrow school
To scare the birds away.

John Carr

The Scarlet Cat

Skill Development

1. Ask the children to name other words beginning with the letter blend *sc*.
2. Read the story together.
   • Focus on the text.
3. Find all the words that begin with *sc*.
   • Write and say these with the children.
   • Check that the children understand the word *scarlet*.

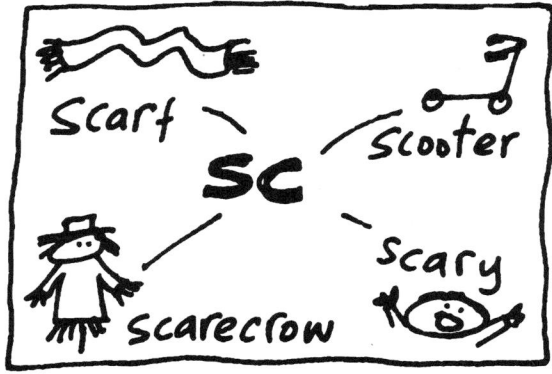

4. Children read the story by themselves.
   • They use the words in the word bank one by one.
   • They read the previously written *sc* chart and illustrate it.
   • Hang the chart up for the children to see.
5. Find the odd-word:
   scarlet, scat, sat.
6. Children make individual booklets.
   • Write a word beginning with *sc* on each page for the children to illustrate.

Writing

1. Children write a story about the scarlet cat on scarlet paper cut into the shape of a cat.
2. Children write and illustrate a new story about the scarlet cat on the computer.
   • Use the published stories to make a class book.
3. Write a class scary book together for children to illustrate.
4. In a shared writing session, write poems using words beginning with *sc*.
   • Put in the class poetry collection.

Develop the story

1. As a shared writing activity, rewrite the ending of the story.
   • Present this as a big book, with the children providing the illustrations.
   • Ask a small group of children to present the story as a play and perform it for the rest of the class.
   • The performers could make simple paper masks of the characters in the story.

A Skeleton Can Skateboard

Skill Development

1. Read the story together.
   - Identify words beginning with *sk* and discuss their meaning.
   - Read again, covering the blend with a mask, asking what the words are.
   - Reread, uncovering the words letter by letter after each blend.
2. Ask the children to think of other words that begin with the same blend.
   - They may suggest words that begin with the same blend of phonemes but with a different graphic representation: for example, *scare* or *scrape*.
   - Praise their efforts, but reinforce that the consonant blends sound the same but they are spelt differently.
   - Write the words up and use them to explain that in English there are spelling choices.
3. Children read the story by themselves.
   - They use the word bank to read the words one by one.
4. Make *sk* words using magnetic letters on a magnetic board.
5. Children illustrate the chart made during the introduction as an independent activity.
6. Find the odd word out: *skip, skate, see; silly, ski, skip.*
7. Look at compound words in the story, e.g. *skate – skateboard, sky – skydive.*
   - Write them on pieces of cardboard.
   - Cut them up.
   - Ask the children to reassemble them.

Writing

1. In a shared writing session write some poems with *sk*: *A skeleton on a skateboard can skydive in a skirt.*
   - Illustrate the rhymes.
   - Paste them on card to use as an independent reading activity.
2. Record missing letter blends on pre-written card or sheet for a cloze-reading task.

   > __ __inny Ned the __ __eleton
   > Is feeling rather thin
   > All he wants for his birthday
   > Is a __ __ateboard
   > And some __ __in.

3. Write individual stories starting with: "I would like to skateboard to…"
   - Write *sk* words on skateboard shape.

Develop the story

1. Make an illustrated concertina chart or frieze.
   - Feature events in sequential order, as in the story.
2. On black paper using white chalk or paint, draw or paint a skeleton and label the bones.
   - Sing the song *Dem bones.*
3. Write instructions on how to use a skateboard.

Words featured

skeleton
skateboard
ski
skip
skittles
skydive
skate
skirt

Poem

Skeleton

Skinny Ned the skeleton
Is feeling rather thin.
All he wants for his
    birthday
Is a skateboard
And some skin.

John Carr

By John Lockyer
illustrations by Jennifer Cooper

Words featured

snoozing
snail
snake
snorkel
snorts
snores
snoozes
sniffles
snuffles
sneezes

Poem

Sniffle. Snuff, Snort

I sniffle and snuff
In the breeze.
I sniffle and snort
Until I sneeze.

John Lockyer

Snoozes And Sneezes

Skill Development

1. Read the title and write it up for the children to see.
   • Check that they understand the word *snooze*.
2. Read the title again emphasising the *sn* blend.
   • Ask the children individually to identify the blend by drawing a circle around the appropriate letters with the whiteboard marker.
3. Read the story together.
   • Focus on the text.
4. Find all the words that begin with *sn*.
   • Write and say these with the children.
   • List them on a chart to be illustrated later.
5. Ask the children for other words beginning with *sn*.
   • Add these to the chart.
   • The chart can be shaped like the blend *sn*.
6. Children read the story by themselves.
   • they use the word bank to read the words one by one.
   • Children read the previously written *sn* chart and illustrate it.
7. Use magnetic letters on a magnetic board to make words beginning with *sn*.
8. Make a "lift the flap" chart to hang up. Ask the children to provide the illustrations.

Writing

1. In a shared writing session ask the children to develop the story.
   • What other objects could the children put on Grandad?
   • Present their ideas in the form of a wall story, with their illustrations.
   • Use the previously made *sn* chart to generate ideas.
2. Ask the children to write a shared poem for the class poetry box.
   • They should use some of the sn words featured in the story.
3. Ask them to write a *sneeze* booklet with a partner .
   • Share with the class or group when completed.
   • Put the finished booklets in the library corner as an independent reading activity.

Develop the story

1. Arrange for a talk from a nurse related to the health issues raised (sneezing and colds).
   • Children draw a self-portrait, complete with a handkerchief or tissue in the pocket.
   • They write a caption in a speech bubble related to the nurse's talk.
2. Encourage children to share a humorous story about their own grandparents.
   • Share the stories orally in a "buzz group", or as written stories.
   • Tape their stories.
3. Make a "snooze" concertina booklet as a group activity.

I Spy A Sparkling Spacecraft

By Susan Frame
Illustrations by Michael Martchenko

Skill Development

1. Read the title slowly, emphasising the *sp* sound.
   • Ask the children what they notice about the words.
   • Ask them to read the title slowly.
2. Talk through the illustrations.
   • Find all the things in the pictures that begin with *sp*.
   • Write the words up as the children say them.
   • Ask the children to read the words slowly with you.
   • Read the story with the children joining in.
3. Children read the story in pairs.
   • Children write the words from the word bank book onto small pieces of cardboard.
   • Working with a friend, the children find and match the cards to the words in the story.
4. Play "I Spy" with the Blend Cards.
   • One child picks up a card and says "I spy a ... crocodile".
   • The other child has to give the correct letter combination of the initial blend to win the card.
   • The child with the most cards at the end of the game is the winner.
5. Look at alliteration and rhyme in the story.

Writing

1. In a Shared Writing Session write an "I Spy" wall story.
   • Children suggest other *sp* things they might spy.
   • Use the same ending as in *I Spy A Sparkling Spacecraft*.
   • Children write a word bank for the wall story of the *sp* words they have used.
   • Children illustrate the wall story.

Develop the story

1. In a shared writing session write some rhymes or poems featuring the *sp* blend with the children.
   • Use the word bank to help.
   • Children illustrate the rhymes.
   • Keep them in a special *sp* box for independent reading.
2. Children make and illustrate concertina books of *sp* words.
   • They use the words from the word bank and from the Blend Card Game to help them.
3. Children write their own "I Spy" booklets.

Words featured

spy
sparkling
spacecraft
speeding
speckled
sparrow
spinach
spoon
spinning
spider
spaghetti
special

Poem

Spaceship

I speed in my spaceship
Towards the sparkling
    stars,
'Til Earth is a speck
As I speed to Mars.

Jane Buxton

Onset Teacher's Notes

By Susan Frame
illustrations by Richard Hoit

Onset Books

Stork Stew

Words featured

stork
starving
sticks
stale
stew
stir
stones
stupendous

Poem

Stone Stew

Stone stew, stone stew,
Stir it with a stick.
Stuff it in a stocking,
And you won't get sick.

Ruth Corrin

Skill Development

1. Write the title up in large letters so the children can see it.
2. Read the written text together, noticing words beginning with *st*.
   • Say the target words slowly and listen to the *s* sound and the *t* sound at the beginning of each.
   • Take care not to distort the individual phonemes.
3. What other words begin with *st*?
   • Write them up so the children can see them.
   • Say the words with the children.
   • Emphasise the beginning sound.
4. Make a word web for the children to illustrate.
5. Play a game using a selection of blend cards.
   • Ask the children: "Can you find the cards that begin with the sounds we hear at the beginning of *stork* and *stew*?"

6. Children read the story by themselves.
   • They use the word bank to read the words one by one.
   • Children listen to the sounds of the words.
7. Children work in pairs to read the story for enjoyment.
   • They say the target words slowly.
   • Check that they are not distorting the phonemes.

Writing

1. Children work together to write some poems for a *Stupendous Stork Stew* Rhyme Book.

> For a stew that tastes stupendous
> We'll stir in sticks,
> some stones, stale bread
> and eat it with a fork!

   • Children read the poems several times as they share in the writing activity.
2. Create a class timeline display with labels and pictures to depict events in the story.
3. Create a stork stew dictionary using words from the word bank.
4. Write a recipe for making Stork Stew.

Develop the story

1. Construct a new story incorporating ideas from children in the class.
   • Children help write target words and letter combinations and illustrate the book.

My Swing

By Jane Buxton
Illustrations by Moira Smith

Onset Books

Skill Development

1. Discuss personal experiences relating to swings.
2. Read the title of the story, emphasising *sw*.
   - Write the title up so the children can see it.
3. Ask what other words begin with *sw*.
   - Write the words in front of the children and say them together.
   - Emphasise the beginning sound.
4. Read the story, emphasising the swinging rhythm.
   - Find all the words that begin with *sw* and write them down.
5. Expand the meaning of the words: for example
   "Show me with your hands how the swallow would swoop."
6. Children read the story by themselves.
   - They use the word bank to read the words one by one.
7. Play "Snap" with the blend cards.
   - Only call "snap" when a *sw* picture or card is turned over.
8. Say a number of words, for example: *swing, song, swan*.
   - Ask children to listen for the odd word out.

Writing

1. Write a new story using the same structure about *Swimming in my Swimming Pool*.
   - Swallows and swans might swim in the pool.
   - Think of a surprise ending.
2. Children use magnetic letters to make as many words as they can that start with *sw*.
   - Children write and illustrate their own personal stories or pages using words from the *sw* word bank.

Develop the story

1. Children illustrate their new swimming stories for a big book.
2. Write up the words using the blend for the children to see.
   - Say each word deliberately and ask the children to point to it or write it down.
   - Make a timeline of the story featuring the main events in sequential order.
   - Draw pictures and write words.

I swing   swallows swoop   swans swim

Words featured

swing
swallows
swooping
swish
swans
swimming
swim

Poem

Sweep

I sweep the streets
With a swishing sound.
I swoosh and I swish
As the street is found!

Clare Scott

By John Carr
Illustrations by Clive Taylor

Chocolate Chomping

Onset Teacher's Notes

Words featured

chomping
children
chomp
chocolate
chew
chimpanzees
cheetahs
chickens
choo

Poem

Chicken and Cheetah

The chicken and the
    cheetah,
Had a cheerful chat,
About chimpanzees,
Chinese cheese,
And Charlie Chipmunk's
    hat.

John Carr

Skill Development

1. Ask the children what they notice about the sound at the beginning of the target words.
   • What letters do they see at the beginning of the target words?
   • Children help write all the words they know that begin with *ch.*
   • Read the story through, emphasising the sound at the beginning of the target words.
2. Children read the story by themselves.
   • They use the word bank to read the words one by one.
   • Children help write the words in the word bank on a chart.
3. Children chant, clap and tap the rhythm patterns of the words and sentences as the book is read.
   • Use the language in the story to create many different chants.
4. Children listen to the sounds of all the words as you say them slowly: *ch–ildren.*
   • Ask what word they hear.
   • Write it down for them to read.

Writing

1. Write a new story around a pyramid of chips, cheese or chocolate chunks.
2. Children make a new word bank for the book.

Develop the story

1. Create a wall display featuring the *ch* sound.

2. Make a recipe involving chocolate.
   • Write the recipe together.
   • Follow the pattern in *Stork Stew*: "We will stir in some ...".
   • Or write a new story: "Stir in some cheese, stir in some chocolate, stir in some ..."
3. Children use a mirror to model themselves eating the chocolate.
   • They draw self-portraits and write a caption. "I am a champion chocolate chunk chewer."
4. Construct an alliterative counting book.
   • Two chocolate chomping children.
     Three chocolate chomping cheetahs...

Mum Takes Us Shopping

Skill Development

1. Children work in small groups. Ask them to:
   - Write words that begin with *sh* on a large sheet of paper.
   - Share their charts with the rest of the class.
2. Write the title up in large letters so the children can see it.
   - Pause for the children to join in the *sh* words.
   - Ask them to read the title slowly emphasising the *sh* sound.
3. Read the story together.
   - Find all the words that begin with *sh*.
   - Talk about their meaning.
4. Children read the story by themselves.
   - They read the words from the word bank and find the words in the story.
   - Listen to the sounds of the words.
5. Create a *sh* word box.
   - Children write and illustrate cards for the box.
6. Ask the children to listen for the odd word out: *shop, shoe, sand.*

Writing

1. Children write and illustrate their own *Mum Takes Us Shopping* booklets, following the pattern of the story.
   - Write word banks of the new words at the end of the booklets.
2. Make up an illustrated shopping list of all the things that begin with *sh*.

Develop the story

1. Use the *sh* words from the stories to make cards for a blend game.
2. Work with the children to write and read tongue-twisters using *sh* words, e.g. *Shayna, shoots, shiny, shells, short, ships, shelly, shines, shimmering.*

Words featured

shopping
shops
shirt
ship
shoes
shells
sheep
shorts
sharks

Poem

Shower

When I have a shower,
My shadow has one too.
My shadow hogs the
    water,
And uses my shampoo.

Belinda M. Thompson

By Clare Scott
Illustrations by Rhian Nest James

Onset Books

Words featured

think
thud
thump
thumb

Poem

Thud, Thud, Thud

There was this thud,
  thud, thud,
Then this flash of light.
There was thunder and
  lightning
Last Thursday night.

Susan Frame

I Think...

Skill Development

1. Ask the children to:
   - Read the story in pairs, reading the words from the word bank.
   - Use magnetic letters to make, break and remake words beginning with *th*.
   - illustrate a *th* chart.
2. Rewrite the text onto light card, folded concertina style.

   - Ask the children to illustrate it, omitting the *th* blend throughout.
   - Make separate blend cards.
   - Ask the children to place in the gaps before reading the story.
3. Ask the children to make patterns of the *th* blend, using crayon, dye or paint.
   - Display around the *th* chart with a selection of books containing the *th* blend.

Writing

1. Write a new story based on *I think I'll build a boat*.
   - Present it as a wall story or enlarged book.
2. Children write a story about their thoughts using thought bubbles.
   - Display on children's self-portraits or on a class mural.
3. In a shared writing session, write some poems using words beginning with *th*.
   - Put them in the class poetry collection.

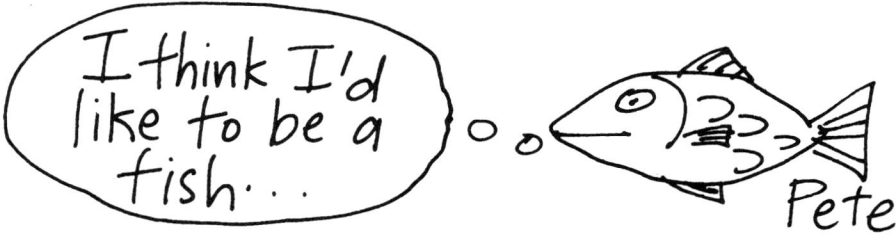

Develop the story

1. Children think about something they could build in the classroom.
2. Children make a thumb puppet out of card or fabric.
   - Children make, observe and compare their thumbprints.

What? When? Where?

Onset Books

wh

By Clare Scott
Illustrations by Dan Schofield

Skill Development

1. Write the title up so the children can see it.
   - Ask children individually to come out and circle the words beginning with *wh*.
2. Read the story together identifying *wh* words.
3. Ask the children for other words that begin with wh.
   - They may suggest words that begin with the same phoneme but with a different spelling, for example *wait, water* etc.
   - Praise their suggestions.
   - Write them down separately to reinforce that they have to make spelling choices.
4. Children read the story by themselves using the word bank to read the words one by one.
5. Make *wh* words using magnetic letters on magnetic board.
   - Make the words then break them up into their sounds.
   - Listen to the sounds of the words.
   - Say the word in sections: *wh–ale*.
   - Children identify the words you are saying.
6. Write the story on strips of cardboard.
   - Cut up the words and reassemble to match the text.

Writing

1. Write a story using the *wh* words on the computer.
   - Illustrate them as a class book and publish.
2. Write a story or poem in a whale shape.

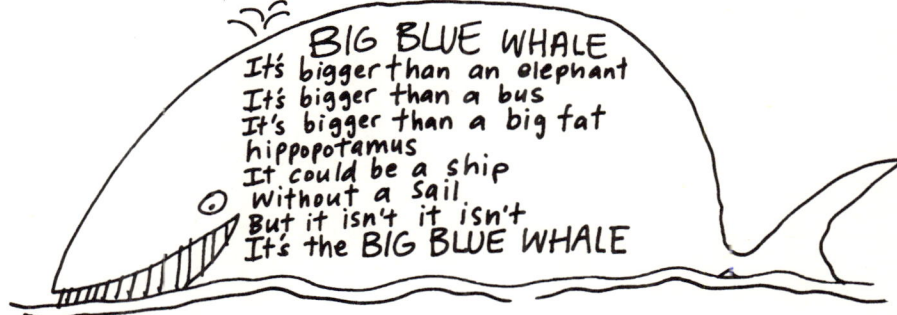

3. Write a class poem inside a *wh* shape. Cut out on cardboard.

Develop the story

1. Role-play the story in groups and present it to the class.
2. Children ask *what, when* and *where* questions about their daily lives and books.
3. Play *what, when, where* games:
   "What have I got in my hand?" " When will we write a story?"
   "Where is Mum?"

Words featured

what
when
where
white
whispered

Poem

Whistle

I whistle when
I'm happy,
I whistle when I'm sad,
I learned to whistle just
   last week,
And, wow – it makes
me glad!

Onset Teacher's Notes

27

br **Brrrr! Brown Bear**

Say each picture name. Circle each picture which begins with the sound **br**.

Do these word sums.

br + icks = _____ .

br + ead = _____ .

br + oom = _____ .

br + idge = _____ .

© Heinemann Educational and Professional Publishing Ltd. Special copyright conditions apply.

cr Crazy Crocodile

Use the letters to make some words.

cr

eep
awl   eek
azy   unch
ocodile

Write them down.

_____ _____ _____

_____ _____ _____

Read the words.
Draw a crazy crocodile.

© Heinemann Educational and Professional Publishing Ltd. Special copyright conditions apply.

 **fr Fruggles**

Write the right word by the pictures. Use the word bank to help you.

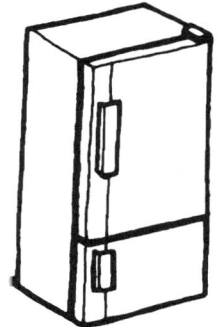

_____   _____   _____

Word bank

Fruggles

fridge

frog

Fred

_____

Which two letters do all the words begin with? ___ ___

Use the word bank to finish the sentence.

There's a _____ in the _____ .

© Heinemann Educational and Professional Publishing Ltd. Special copyright conditions apply.

 **Granny Green**

Match the picture to the words.
Write the words.

growling _____   Granny Green

_____   growling

_____   Grandpa Green

_____   grapes

_____   grinning

Draw the pictures.

I am grinning.	I am growling.

© Heinemann Educational and Professional Publishing Ltd. Special copyright conditions apply.

Draw things that begin with *tr* in the triangle.

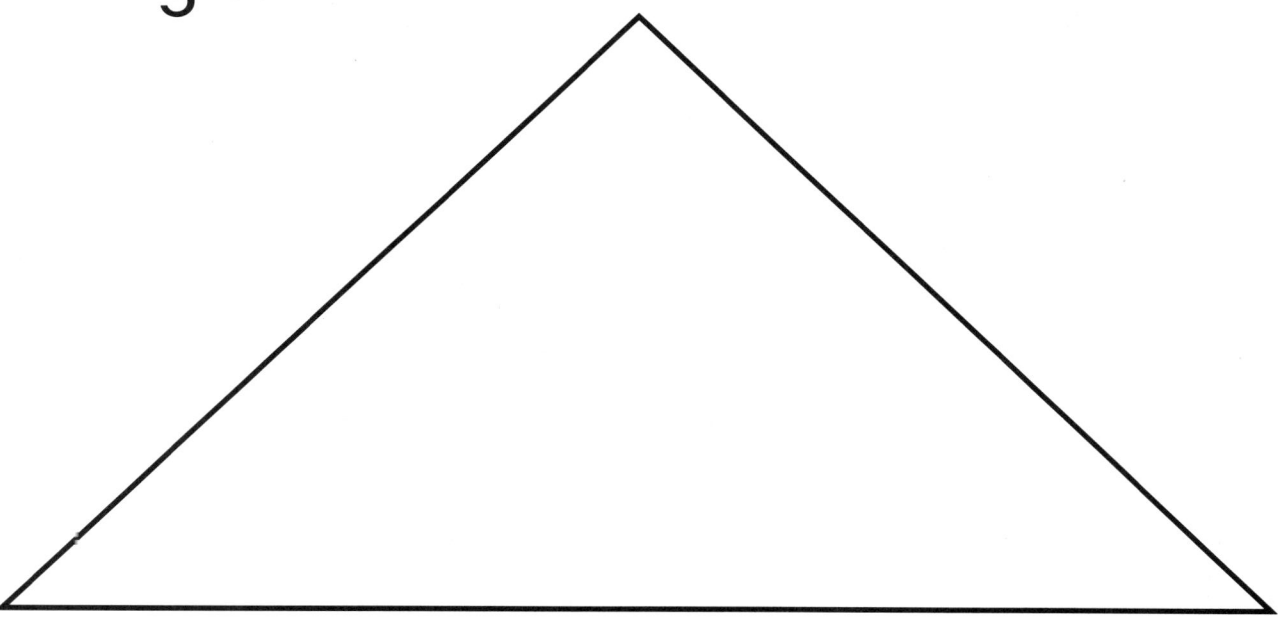

Use words beginning with tr to finish the sentences.

I try to climb a _____ .

I try to drive a _____ .

I try to play the _____ .

Some words to help you

trumpet   tree   tractor

© Heinemann Educational and Professional Publishing Ltd. Special copyright conditions apply.

 **Cloudland**

Use the letters to make words beginning with *cl*.

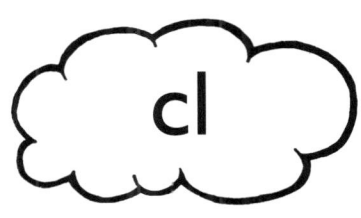

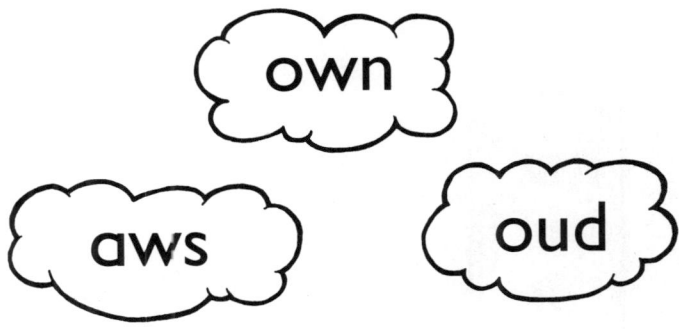

Write them by the right picture.

Finish the sentences. Use your words.

I see a funny _____ .

I can see the _____ .

I see a cat with _____ .

© Heinemann Educational and Professional Publishing Ltd. Special copyright conditions apply.

fl **Flop, Flap, Flip**

SUNSHINE BOOKS

Use the letters to make words beginning with **fl**.

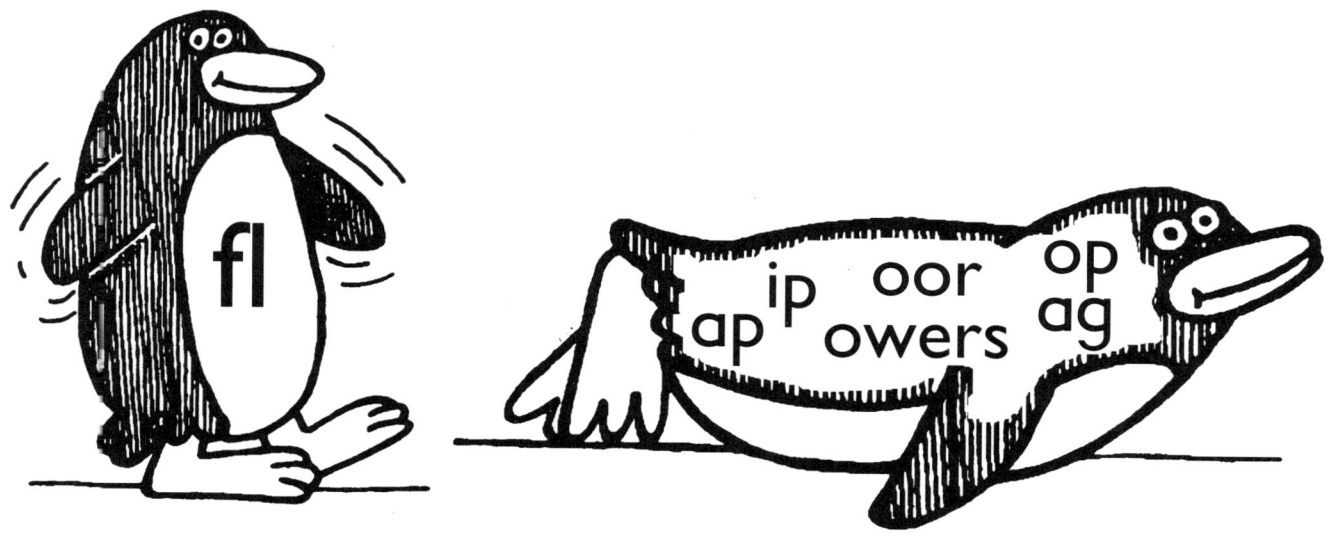

Write the words you have made on the flower.

Read them.

© Heinemann Educational and Professional Publishing Ltd. Special copyright conditions apply.

gl Glueing My Glider

Colour all the pictures that begin with **gl**.

Finish these sentences.
Use the word bank to help you.

There's ____ on my _____ .

There's ____ on my _____ .

There's ____ on my _____ .

Word bank
gloves   glue   glider   glasses

© Heinemann Educational and Professional Publishing Ltd. Special copyright conditions apply.

pl The Mouse Plays With The Plane

Circle all the words that begin with *pl*.

x	p	l	a	y	s	s	h
p	l	u	m	d	p	o	t
j	n	f	p	l	a	n	t
e	p	l	a	n	k	r	b
f	c	p	l	a	t	e	m
p	l	a	n	e	e	l	j
y	m	d	a	p	l	u	g
p	l	e	a	s	e	z	k

Write them down.

_____   _____   _____

_____   _____

Read them to a friend.

© Heinemann Educational and Professional Publishing Ltd. Special copyright conditions apply.

 **A Slimy Slug**

Write **sl** to finish the words.

__ __ ug   __ __ ide   __ __ ipper

__ __ eeping   __ __ eeve

Use the words you have made.
Write them by the correct picture.

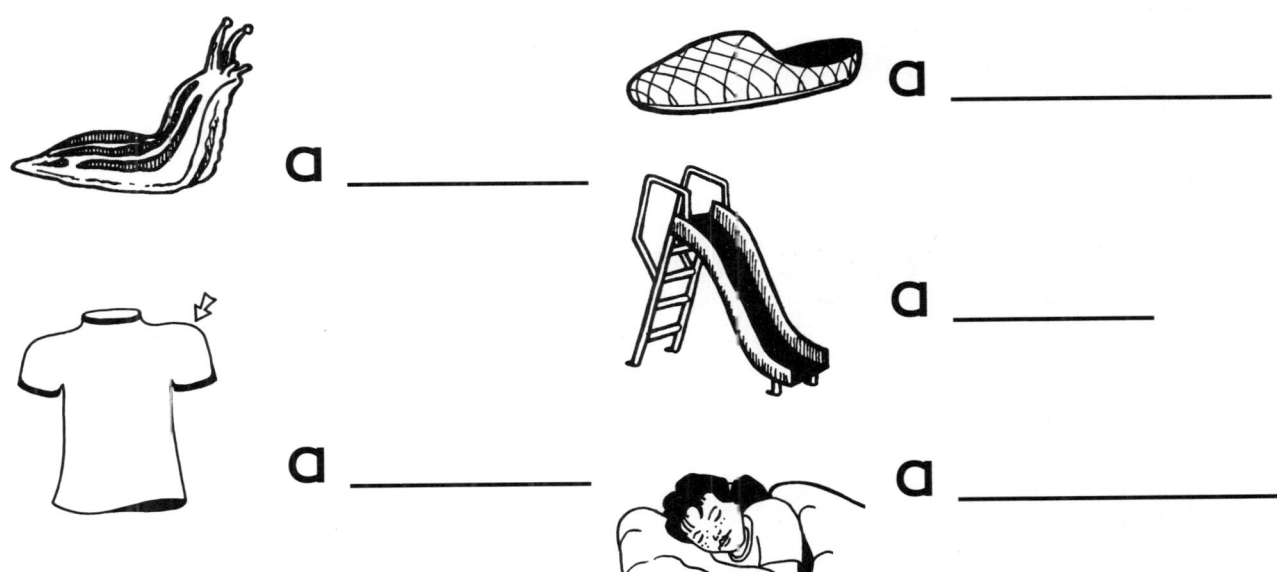

a _____

a _____

a _____

a _____

a _____

a _____
_____

Draw a slimy slug on your sleeve!

© Heinemann Educational and Professional Publishing Ltd. Special copyright conditions apply.

sc The Scarlet Cat

Write **sc** by all the pictures that begin with those letters. Use the word bank to help you.

Word bank

scarecrow

scarf

scooter

screw

Write two things the boy said to the cat.

I am _____
_____ _____

_____
_____
_____ !

© Heinemann Educational and Professional Publishing Ltd. Special copyright conditions apply.

 # A Skeleton Can Skateboard

Write the sentences. Use the word bank to help you.

Word Bank
skeleton
ski
skateboard
A
can

_ _ _ _ _ _ _ _ _ _

_ _ _ _ _ _ _ _

Draw your own picture about the skeleton.
Write a sentence.

© Heinemann Educational and Professional Publishing Ltd. Special copyright conditions apply.

 **Snoozes And Sneezes**

Cut out the tiles.
Use them to make words beginning with **sn**.
Write the words you make.

| sn | ap | eeze |
| ip | ow | ooze |

| ake | iff |
| ail | ack |

© Heinemann Educational and Professional Publishing Ltd. Special copyright conditions apply.

sp I Spy A Sparkling Spacecraft

What can you spy beginning with **sp**?
Use the word bank to help you.

I spy a _____ .

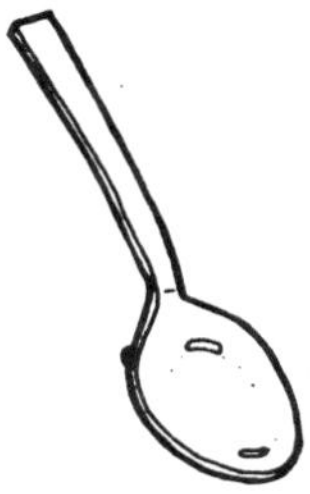

I spy a _____ .

I spy _____ .

I spy a _____ .

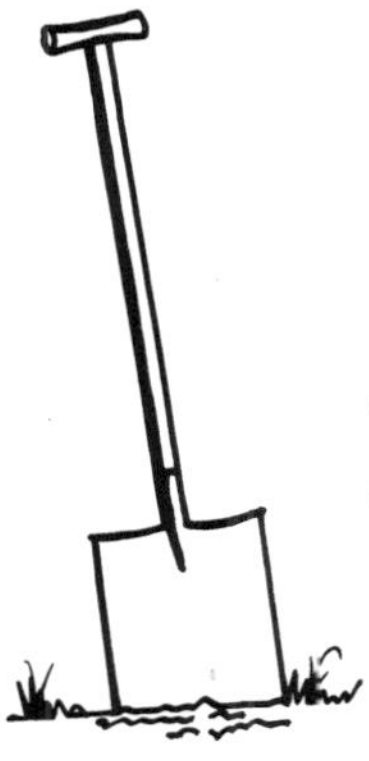

I spy a _____ .

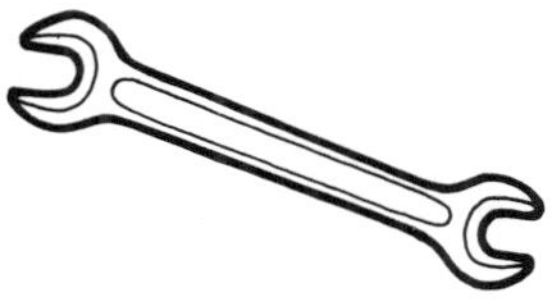

I spy a _____ .

Word bank		
spacecraft	spider	spoon
spaghetti	spanner	spade

© Heinemann Educational and Professional Publishing Ltd. Special copyright conditions apply.

st Stork Stew

Use the letter stew to make words beginning with **st**.

ring

icks

ones

ars

alks

amps

raw

Use the words you have made to write a new recipe for stork stew.

Stork Stew
You need:

_____

_____

_____

_____

_____

© Heinemann Educational and Professional Publishing Ltd. Special copyright conditions apply.

Join the letters. Match to the pictures.

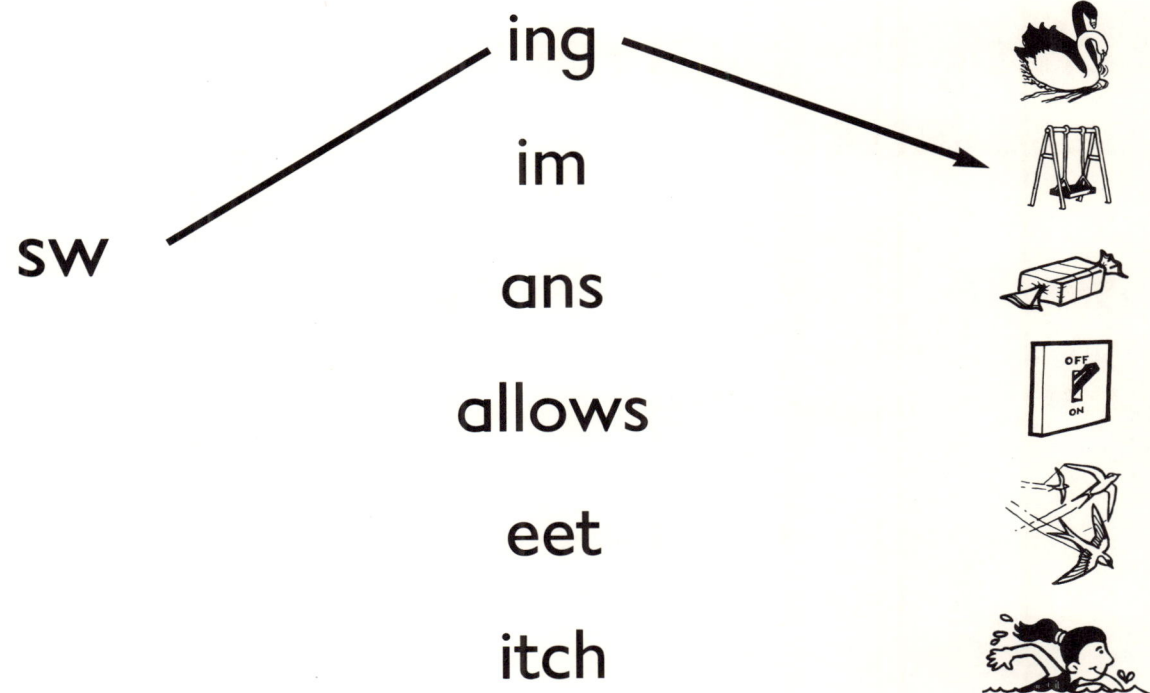

sw

ing

im

ans

allows

eet

itch

Finish the sentences.

I see _____ .

I see a _____ .

I see _____ .

I see a _____ .

I see a _____ .

© Heinemann Educational and Professional Publishing Ltd. Special copyright conditions apply.

ch Chocolate Chomping

SUNSHINE BOOKS

Write **ch** by the pictures that begin with those letters.

What noise did the children make when they chewed the chocolate?

© Heinemann Educational and Professional Publishing Ltd. Special copyright conditions apply.

 **Mum Takes Us Shopping**

Use the letters to make words beginning with **sh**.

sh

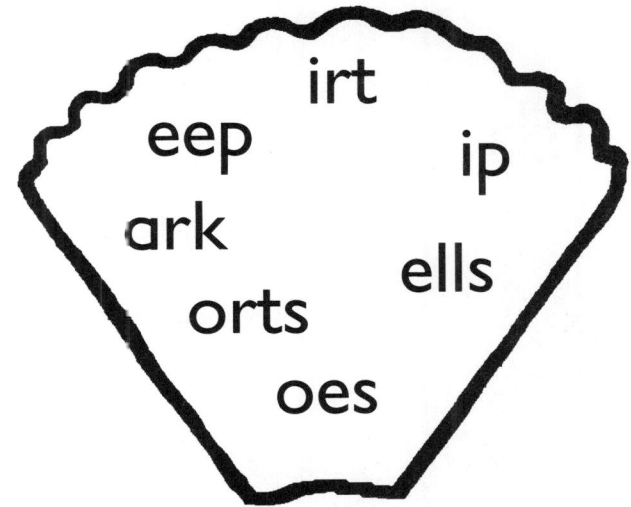

irt
eep
ark
orts
oes
ip
ells

Use the words to finish Mum's shopping list.

Shopping List

 A _____ with a _____ on it.

 _____ with a _____ on them.

A sweater with _____ on it.

 _____ with _____ on them.

© Heinemann Educational and Professional Publishing Ltd. Special copyright conditions apply.

th I think ...

Use the letters to make words beginning with **th**.

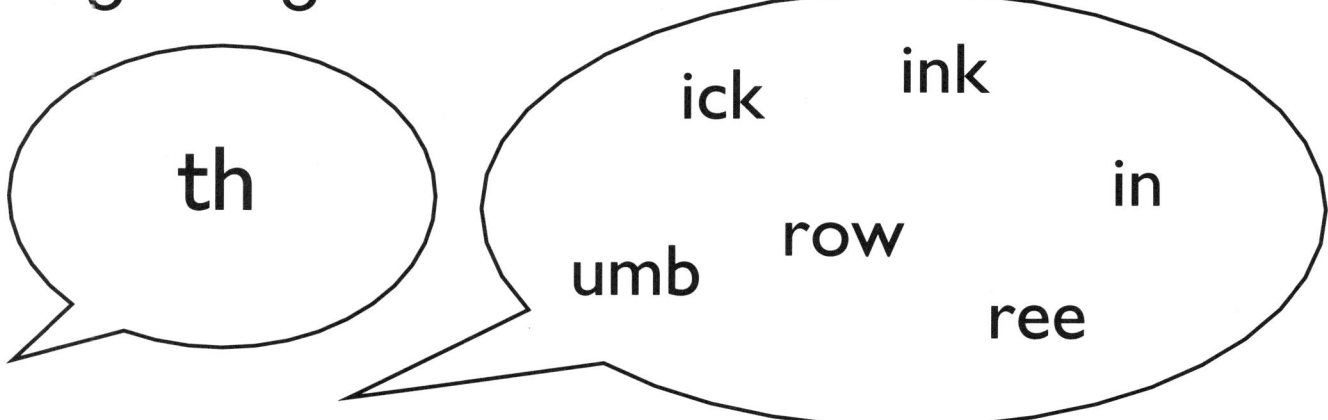

th

ick   ink

in

umb   row

ree

Write your words by the correct picture.

3 _____

_____

_____

_____

Draw three thumbs.

© Heinemann Educational and Professional Publishing Ltd. Special copyright conditions apply.

wh **What? When? Where?**

The children ask Mrs White lots of
questions. Write them.
Use the word bank to help you.

when who
why
where
what
which

© Heinemann Educational and Professional Publishing Ltd. Special copyright conditions apply.

Letter Blend Knowledge recording grid

Name:

_____

Date:

_____

	S	W	SE		S	W	SE
bl				sc			
br				sh			
ch				sk			
cl				sl			
cr				sm			
dr				sn			
fl				sp			
fr				st			
gl				sw			
gr				th			
pl				tr			
pr				wh			

Key:
S: Sound
W: Word
SE: Sentence

Comments:

Onset Teacher's Notes